First published in Great Britain
by Pendulum Gallery Press
56 Ackender Road Alton
Hants GU34 1JS

Why SHOPPING is
better then SEX

ISBN 0-948912-38-3

PRINTED 1998
PRINTED IN GREAT BRITAIN BY
UNWIN BROTHERS LTD, OLD WOKING, SURREY

TO JANET BAKER, WITHOUT WHO'S HELP, THIS BOOK
WOULD HAVE BEEN FINISHED A LOT EARLIER...
BUT WITH NOT SUCH GOOD IDEAS...

Shopping is better than Sex because....

You can do it riding whatever you like...

Shopping is
better
than Sex
because....

You can get
personal
satisfaction
EVERY time...

Shopping is
better
than Sex
because....

You can do it
as many times
during the day
as YOU like...

Shopping is
better
than Sex
because....

You can do it
wherever
YOU choose...

Shopping is
better
than Sex
because....

You can have
something to
eat while
you're doing
it...

Shopping is
better
than Sex
because....

You don't
have to
make the bed
afterwards...

Shopping is
better
than Sex
because....

You can go up
and down as
many times
as YOU like...

Shopping is
better
than Sex
because....

You can get
100%
attention
all the time...

Shopping is
better
than Sex
because....

You know
what you're
going to get
before you
start...

Shopping is
better
than Sex
because....

If you don't
like it, you can
take it back...

Shopping is
better
than Sex
because....

If you see
something you
like, you can
take it home
with you...

Shopping is
better
than Sex
because....

You can pay
for it with your
husband's
credit card...

Shopping is
better
than Sex
because....

You can do it
without having
to talk dirty...

Shopping is
better
than Sex
because....

You can chat
with a friend
while doing
it...

Shopping is
better
than Sex
because....

You can do it
when the
children are
at school...

Shopping is
better
than Sex
because....

You can do it
without having
to listen to
your husband
complaining...

Shopping is better than Sex because....

You can do it without having to listen to your husband's jokes...

Shopping is
better
than Sex
because....

You can
do it in a
different way
every time...

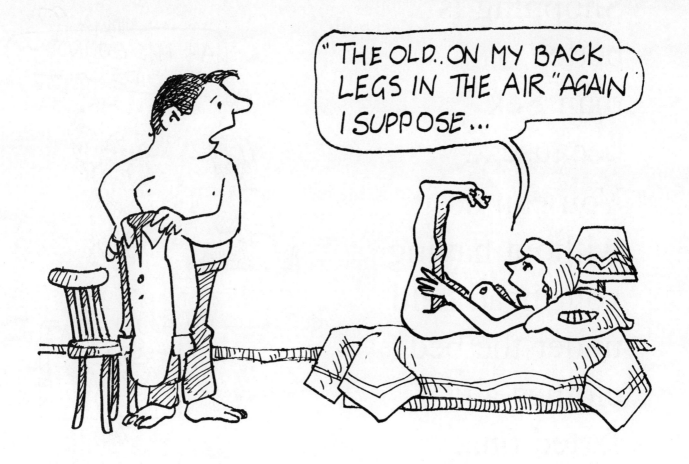

Shopping is better than Sex because....
You can do it without having your head held under the bed-clothes and farted on...

Shopping is
better
than Sex
because....

You can
stop it,
whenever
YOU like...

Shopping is
better
than Sex
because....

You can do it
anyway
YOU like...

Shopping is
better
than Sex
because....

You can do it
wearing
whatever
YOU like...

Shopping is
better
than Sex
because.....

You can stop
and sit down if
you're getting
out of breath...

Shopping is better than Sex because....

You don't have to take the family pets with you...

Shopping is
better
than Sex
because....

You can do it
as much as
you like,
whatever age
you are...

Shopping is better than Sex because....

You can do it without having to get up and make the tea afterwards...

Shopping is
better
than Sex
because....

You can
sit on
whatever
YOU like...

Shopping is
better
than Sex
because....

You can eat
whatever
YOU like...

Shopping is better than Sex because....

You can do it and drink as much as you like...

Shopping is
better
than Sex
because....

You can do it
without having
to wait for your
partner to come
back from the
pub...

Shopping is
better
than Sex
because....

You don't
have to wear
a condom...

Shopping is
better
than Sex
because....

You can
do it
on your own...